THIS POEM is a NEST

THIS POEM

is a

NEST

Irene Latham   art by **Johanna Wright**

WORDSONG

AN IMPRINT OF BOYDS MILLS & KANE

New York

For Rebecca Davis,
best nest-building partner ever
—IL

For my birdies,
Juniper and Billy Robin
—JW

Wordsong
An imprint of Boyds Mills & Kane, a division of Astra Publishing House
wordsongpoetry.com

Printed in the United States of America

ISBN: 978-1-68437-363-5 (hc) • 978-1-63592-430-5 (eBook)
Library of Congress Control Number: 2019953794

First edition
10 9 8 7 6 5 4 3 2 1

Design by Barbara Grzeslo
The text is set in Frutiger.
The titles are set in Brush Up.
The illustrations are done digitally with ink washes.

INTRODUCTION

One day when I was watching robins build a nest, it occurred to me that poems are nests—and we poets spend much of our time nest-building. We gather words, ideas, and dreams, and then we set about weaving, arranging, and structuring.

The birds outside my window wove their nest to hold eggs and, eventually, nestlings. This book was created in much the same way: first I wove the "nest" or source poem, and then I started searching for "nestlings"—the name I've given the small poems nesting inside the big poem titled "Nest," which you'll find on the next pages.

Nestling poems are simply a variation of "found" poems. Found poems are created by looking at an existing source text (for example, a story or article) and selecting words that make sense to you. It's rather like a game of seek-and-find! The only rule is that the words or parts of words in your poem must appear in the same order that they do in the original text. (Another type of found poetry is "blackout" poetry, a technique often used with newspaper or magazine articles in which you black out all the words that you've decided *not* to use, highlighting only the ones you want.)

Nestling poems are distinguished by the fact that they are found within a *poem*—and in the case of this book, the nest poem and the nestlings are all a single poet's work. The challenge of this project for me was to find as many different kinds of nestlings as possible. Also, I wanted to use every single word in the nest at least once—which meant in the end finding a total of 161 nestling poems! The last word to find a home? *Cold*. The most often used word? *Sky*. Sometimes

I had to find a stray *s* to make a verb tense work. What fun to play with words, to arrange and rearrange, and to watch some of them learn to fly!

You can use "Nest" to write your own poems, or you can use any other poem. You'll probably find—as I did—that some words will call to you more insistently, or are simply more versatile. You can put these words to use in different nestlings, in different contexts, sometimes with quite different meanings. Because we are all unique individuals, an infinite number of unique nestlings might be found in a single poem. Remember, too, that titles are one area where you can be particularly imaginative, because they need not be found inside the source poem. Who knew there was a poem about Mars inside a poem titled "Nest"?

What words will call to you?

What worlds are waiting in a poem for

you to discover? What ideas are hiding

that you—and only you—

will nurture until they're ready

to fly right out of the nest into a

new poem?

–IL

CONTENTS

PART 1

NEST

NEST

I. Spring

This poem has twigs in it, and little bits of feather-fluff.
It's got wings and birdsong stitched together with ribbons of hope.
Safe in its crook, it's a cradle that sways across day and dark.

Whatever the weather, leafy choir rustles a lullaby.
By miracle or fate, the fragile eggs stay snug in their cup—
blue gemstones precious as any long-buried pirate's plunder.

Soon there are *peep-peep-peep*s and beaks that hinge open-shut-open.
The happy nest overflows with flap-flapping and endless feast.
Nestlings become fledglings. They share first falls and fluttery flights.

II. Summer

New adventures call, and, one by one, the robins wing away.
Off they fly past sun and moon, tiny stars in vast seaglass sky.
Empty nest becomes nothing more than a morning house of light.

Just below, monarch butterfly expands damp, delicate wings.
Spider weaves a glittery web, and green tree frog trills a tune.
Honeybees buzz past the nest, fuzzy legs coated in gold-dust.

Can you hear the oak thrumming, *Welcome*? Grey squirrels chattering,
Let's play? Crickets chirp-chirping *Come find me* as they wait to mate?
In this poem, there's a home for everything—even you.

III. Autumn

Won't you breathe, reach? Grab hold and climb these branches like a
    ladder—
up and up—where the crispcool world turns both smaller and bigger.
From here shipwrecked nest shows moorings; settles into hull, deck, mast.

Distant woodsmoke seasons air as dizzy leaves flood forest floor.
Three deer take the stage below, sniff, then swerve in sudden ballet.
When a box turtle splashes into a sunpuddle, clouds still.

Time now to imagine another life: wings and wordless flight;
the whisperweight of faith tucked beneath an acorn's jaunty hat;
near-naked oak hums with ancient memory as you drop down.

IV. Winter

Frost-kissed limbs glimmer in cold moonlight, shiver a rattlesong.
When white-footed mouse discovers nest, it makes needed repairs:
adds grassy roof, stocks walls with sweet arsenal of nuts and seeds.

Busy mouse doesn't stop between naps to ask *why?* or *what for?*
Like tiger beetle, it cruises wrinkly oakbark despite chill—
sails forth into wild cathedral of forest, heartbeat, and sky.

This poem has twigs in it, and little bits of feather-fluff.
It's got feet and mouse-squeak stitched together with ribbons of hope.
Safe in its harbor, it's both wise anchor and dreamworthy boat.

Come now—won't you climb inside?

PART II

NESTLINGS

POEMS TO MARK THE DAY

Dawn

day rustles open,
overflows
morning boat

Lunchtime

in it together
nestlings
chirp
a poem

Afternoon Lull

safe cradle
of light—
　　　　wordflight!

Dusk

sky weaves
gold-dust;
world
      turns

Bedtime

you drop
down
in moonsong—
ask sky:
got dreams?

Middle-of-the-Night Question

wing away,
or take
the stage?

Another Middle-of-the-Night Question

what stays?
anything?

CALENDAR POEMS

January

dark lullaby—

fragile
      light

expands
wrinkly sky

February

nothing
green—

everything
on hold

March

day flap-flapping
empty tune—
crispcool air
rattles roof

April

chirping sun
with little bits
of hope
inside

May

birdsong season—
leaves glimmer,
grass doesn't
stop

June

endless feast
of light—

splash!
drop anchor!

July

choir of crickets
whisper,
hum
as you sail
forth

August

song sways,
flaps past stars—

time, a heartbeat

September

grab hat—sail
into harbor,
won't you?

October

sky shipwrecked,
oak like
a wild dream

November

blue stars thrum—
time to drop
a tiger
into sky

December

welcome home!

busy hearts
stitched together—

safe inside

SEASON POEMS, OR "NEST," ABRIDGED

Note: These nestlings were found only within the section of their subject. So, for example, "Spring" below contains only words from the "Spring" section of "Nest."

Spring

got wings?

soon, open
nest—

first flights!

Summer

sky, empty—

nothing more
than weave,
trill, buzz—

they wait for you

Autumn

world settles,
leaves puddle—

still, time hums

Winter

frostsong
whitechill
skydream
you

BEFORE & AFTER POEMS

Before the Announcement

happy morning thrumming—

grab hold
as dizzy clouds
drop down

After the Announcement

wings shut
no chattering
everything swerves—

clouds stop

Before the Storm

new web—
whisper-kissed,
stitched harbor

After the Storm

little bits of light—
spider finds
wrecked life

Before the Game

hope sways—
becomes
fluttery

After the Game Is Won

away they fly!

stars buzz
up and up—
don't stop

After the Game
Is Lost

hope
smoke now

Red

autumn leaves
puddle
beneath roof
of sky

Orange

imagine
a tiger's
wild heart

Yellow

honeybees thrum,
welcome home

Green

nothing more
than a forest

Blue

vast sea—a home
for everything

Indigo

song of
sky and ink

Violet

morning's
glittery web
coated in
woodsmoke

Brown

day trills a tune
of acorn
nuts
oakbark

White

clouds drop kisses,
sail forth
wise and worthy

Black

dark splash
whispers
ancient glimmersong

POEMS ABOUT WiLD ANiMALS

Herd of Alpaca in the Rain

snug in their
fuzzy coats,
they wait
for another
sky

Octopus on the Prowl

has piratebeak

flows in
endless sea

becomes both
smaller
and bigger

Peacock Parade

it's got
flap-flapping
seaglass wings—

a glittery flood
of feathers

Caterpillar Dreams of Flight

safe in its cradle,
fuzzy legs turn
to smoke

Upside-Down Sloth

sways across day,
whatever the weather—

and waits

and

and—

    still

Portrait of Papa Emperor Penguin with Egg

feet stitched
together,
both anchor
    and dream

Lion, Late Afternoon

fluff of gold
needs
arsenal of naps

Owl Calling
on a Moonless Night

let me
      you   you

    hold
         you you

LEARNING-FROM-WILDLIFE POEMS

How to Hang in There

spider waits—
makes needed repairs,
doesn't stop

The Benefits of Compromise

crickets find a ladder
between bark
and squeak—
safe now

There Is a Time to Dance and a Time to Be Still and Watch the Dancers

dizzy deer—
                frost-footed—
stop heart

The Power of Imagination

turtle tucked in moonlight
makes cathedral
inside

The Power of Song

dark weather—
frogs honeybuzz still!

what ribbons
      of hope

What to Do When You Know Something Is Wrong

mouse
squeaks

What to Do When Boredom Sets In

squirrels play
find the sun—

now acorns
glimmer

What to Do When You Are Lost

honeybees climb,

swerve—

discover poem
safe inside

When You Are Feeling Hopeless, Look Up

soon
butterfly wings
splash sky,
stitch dream

All You Need, According to a Snail

tiny home—

floor
       roof
walls

          heart

ANIMAL STORY POEMS

Hatching Story

miracle eggs
hinge open—

flap-flap

damp ballet
to an ancient song

Hidden Treasure Story

this poem has gemstones,
pirates and feast

glittery gold
    and a ladder—

time now to stop,
ask, *why mouse-squeak?*

Kraken Story

choir of ships
swerves into a cloud
beneath cold moon

Story of a Little Chick Lost

peep!
peep!

where's Ma?

so dizzy . . .

then,
wings!

(and kisses)

Tornado Story

limbs rattle;
beetle cruises

Windfall Story

can you hear
squirrels sniff,
then whisper
a jaunty song?

Tadpoles' Close-Call Story

bird
peep-peeps,

lights
past

thrumming
puddle

Story of an Egg in Three Parts

I
cradle

II
shipwreck

III
memory

HUMAN

EMOTION POEMS

Fear

long-buried
chatter
turns tiger
into mouse

Lonely

Dark fate:
moon becomes
grey—
distant
　　　　as faith

Heartbroken

open-shut-open heart
has twigs in it now

Annoyed

little stones
flap-flap—
nothing trills

Depressed

day
becomes
a tiger

Grief

dark season
when time
won't climb

What Hope Is

a cup
of stars

Faith

ancient heartbeat
of hope

Joy

it's got wings,
stars,
dizzy sun

Vulnerable

sudden splash—

clouds naked
as moonlight

Brave Poem

you climb
into wild
        boat

Proud Poem

cradle
of sun
becomes a home
for you

Mad Poem

world
a box

Confused Poem

with that
or
as that?

in
or
in to?

This poem
is
      you!

When You're Happy

poemsky
expands—
you climb
up and up,
settle
into sun

RELATIONSHIP POEMS

Best Friends

together,
    snug—

they share
    stars

Disagreement Poem

dark rustle,
fluttery dust—

time stops

Parent Poem

this poem
has endless
faith
in you

When You Meet Your New Teacher

you hear, *welcome!*
let's play!

you breathe—

world bigger,
still safe

New Kid's Plea

welcome me,
won't you?

"Cool" Kids,
According to an Outsider

little crooks,
they buzz past—
another wordless winter

Team Practice

one sky—
light thrumming—
time, a song

Resentment

a long-buried
nothing

Remembering the One Who Went Away

stones call,
breathe—

settle into
weight
of memory

Crush

crisp season
splashes down
a song,
adds sky

Rejection

it's got
winter
in it

Peace Offering

twig of birdsong,
ribbon of stars,
butterfly wings

Forgiveness

little miracle,
delicate trill—

you find moorings

POEMS FOR FUN AND FULFILLMENT

Reading

happy adventure,
nothing more than
words tucked
in light

Running

off they fly—
heart's got feet

Rock Climbing

breathe
    reach
        hold—
climb ladder
into clouds

Dancing

wordless flight
of heartbeat
and feet

Playing the Trumpet

glittery trill,
gold thrum—
splashsong!

Archery

feather's
got wings—
buzz

Boating

sea trills,
welcome, mates!
sail forth!

Painting

ribbons of blue
become star-sky—

delicate world
shows another
you

Gaming

adventures call:
let's play!

you grab world
beneath roof, walls—

cruise inside

Watching a Sunset

blue
becomes
butter

Volunteering for a Cause

busy poem's
got *together* in it

FOR the
LOVE
of
WORDS

ALPHABET POEMS

Note: To create these nestlings, I first combed "Nest" to find words beginning with the same letter. Next, I imagined a subject beginning with that letter, and then I included only the words that still made sense.

F Is for Falcon

fragile
flap-flapping
fledglings—

first falls,
fluttery flights—

fly!

find flood,
forest

H Is for Hive

hope hinges
happy house—

honeybees hear

home!
   heart!
      harbor!

S Is for Shipwreck

snug stones

soon share
summer sun,

stars, sea—

ship settles,
splashes

shivers—
stops

W Is for White Ibis

wings—
        whatever
        weather—
                wings!

wings weave,
        wait
        where world's wordless,
                white
                wrinkly
                        wild

                                wise

WORDPLAY POEMS

Double, Double Toil and Trouble (Witch's Brew)

poemfluff
robinwing
flyweave
frogbuzz
squirrelchirp
deerswerve
turtlesplash
mousenap
beetlebeat
poemhope

Sneeze Poem

it's
   it's
      it's
         it's   you!

DEFINITION POEMS

A Definition of Yes

day flows,
expands—
everything
glimmers

A Definition of No

song
stitched
shut

Another Definition of No

chatter-rattle
stops—
you climb

A Definition of Maybe

hinge between
wild
and safe

POEMS OF VIEWS AND VISTAS

Desert

one moon
for everything
whispers, *come*—

Meadow

feathersong
sways a lullaby

Cave

dark house—
damp hull,
or ancient
cathedral?

Fog

precious sun
coated in
arsenal of feather-fluff

Cherry Trees in Bloom

wings,
sky-buzz—
world
puddles
white

Iceberg

glass house
glimmer-shivers—
wild anchor

Mountain Streams in Love

they fall
        flutter
           trill—

flood together

Abandoned Farm

weathered wood
whispers,
harbor inside

Fox Den

safe world
tucked
beneath moon

AROUND-THE-WORLD POEMS:
A VISIT TO THE SEVEN
CONTINENTS AND BEYOND

African Serengeti

Turtle-sun
puddles
in grassy
cathedral

Antarctica's
Lambert Glacier

overflows below:
white walls,
wild harbor

Northern Lights

blue-green
shipwreck sky
with ribbons

At the Top of Mount Everest

hold world—
imagine flight,
discover
arsenal of hope

Australian Outback

empty,
everything
distant—
time naps

Germany's Black Forest

dark lullaby
buried under moon
drops seeds,
despite chill

North America's Great Plains

nothing but
gold grass
stitched with
dreams

Tahiti

little bit of stone
in endless sea—

sweet sails
anchor you

Amazon River

flows past
seasons—

swerves,
splashes—

life,
a ribbon

SPACE POEMS

Sun's Complaint

near-ancient moon
rattles
when it dreams

When People Forget the Planet Closest to the Sun (Mercury)

tiny monarch
doesn't
squeak

The Case for Sending Probes to Venus

woodsmoke clouds
glimmer
with little bits
of hope

Earth

green thrumming
poem-ship
sails wild sky

Mars Landing

breath settles—

dizzy time!

life hums
as you drop
anchor

Jupiter

pirate moons
shiver
between *why?*
and sky

Saturn's Rings

ribbons of stone
coated in
gold-dust
and smoke

Uranus

crook-cradle
snug in web,
where crispcool
clouds nap

As Neptune Turns

blue house—
distant glimmer
in shiver-sky

On Pluto No Longer Being Named a Planet

It's an itch:
dark stone nest
becomes
nothing

Stellar Nursery

cradle
overflows
with naked
hope

Constellations Calling

ribbons of light
thrumming, *now,*
come now

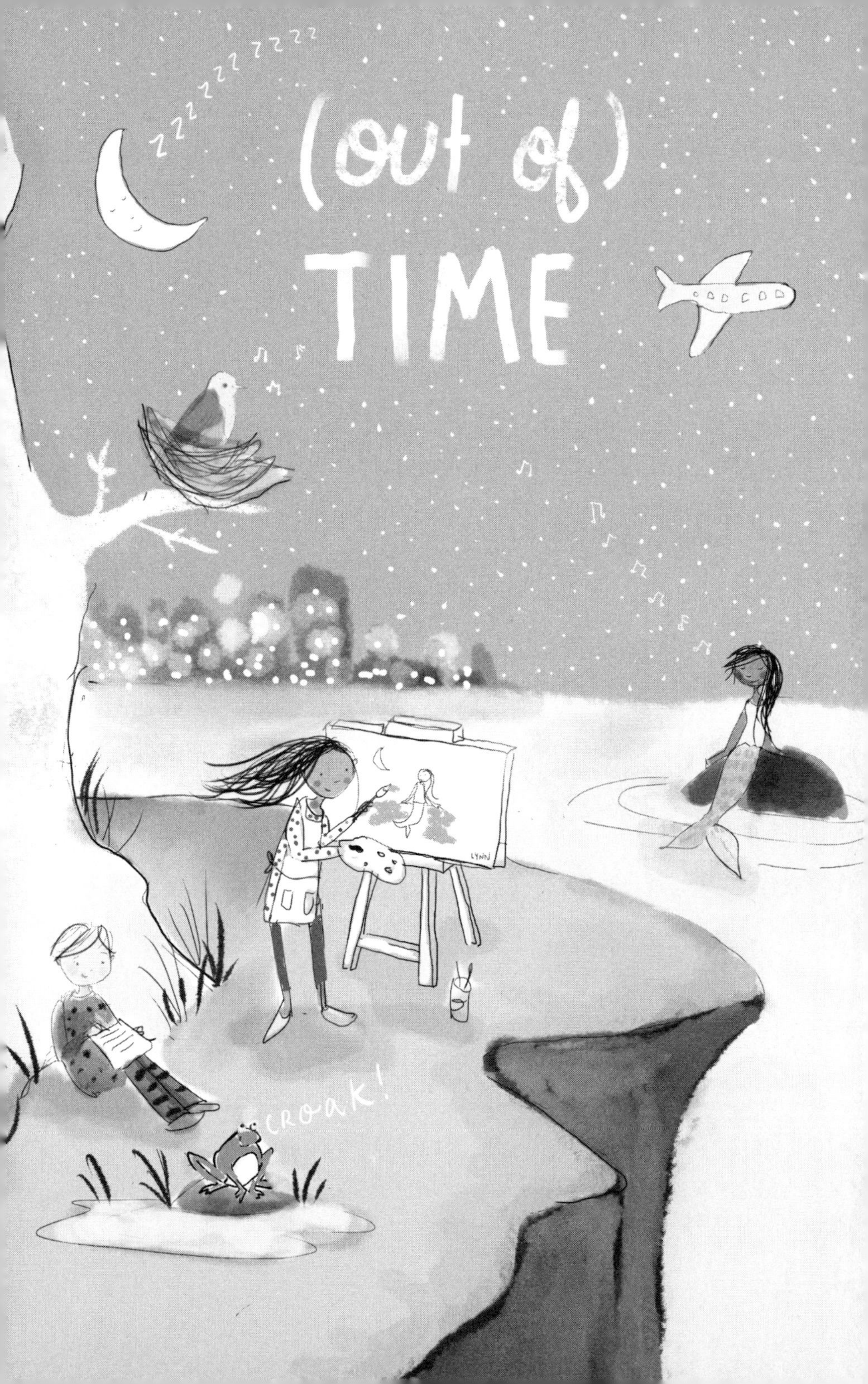
(out of)
TIME
LYNN
croak!

ARS POETICA

Poem's Siren Song

come below
to hear
sky
inside

Going on a Poem Hunt

first mate
climbs ladder—

from here
ship shows
deck, mast,
sails—

skyboat

What You Might Discover
If You Write a Poem about a Tree

what?
branches *like* nests?
the weight
adds
    hope?

Where You'll Find Me
on a Flyaway Day

in
oak branches
where words
and art
anchor me

First Poem-Draft

ink squeaks
with hope

Question to Ask While Writing

this poem:
feast,
or fluff?

Because
Inspiration Is Everywhere

spring is leafy
plunder—
there are robins,
sun,
      green trees—

on the forest floor,
three jaunty
feathers

Poem Found
While Looking at the City
from an Airplane Window
at Night

miracle star
just below you—
cool nest
of lights

This Poet's Mind, When Not Writing

and and
          the nest
and and
          the nest

and the nest

the
      this
              there—

      and the nest!

What a Poem *Should* Be

a feather-stitched
hinge—

open-shut-open—

endless flight!

a home
        for the world

While You Sleep

moon
stocks poems
with dreams

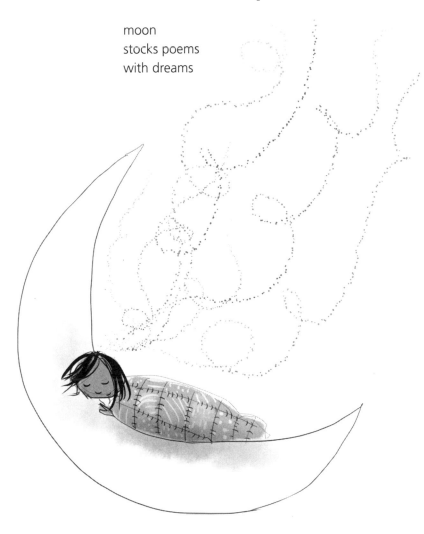

After a
Dark and Stormy Night

by morning
web trills—
as world turns,
poems climb
inside

Miracle

by frog!
even these splashes
puddle poems

FiNAL THoUGHTS

My Wish for You

blue adventure
in seaglass morning—

green buzz,
gold thrumming—

life
      a poem

Last Poem

birdsong,
nothing more

TIPS FROM A NEST-BUILDER: HOW TO FIND NESTLINGS

1. Choose your nest carefully.

It's true that poems are everywhere. But you'll find the most interesting nestlings in nest-poems that include rich language. Look for nests that give you lots of powerful and versatile words to choose from.

2. Begin your search.

Here are some ways to get started:

Select one word.

Choose a word near the top of the nest that calls to you. Next, write it down, circle it, use a highlighter to highlight it, or simply "eyeball" it. Now build your poem by selecting the next word that goes with your first word. Keep going until you have a chain of several words that make sense to you.

Choose a subject first.

Decide what you want to write about—maybe it's an animal, or a place. Comb the poem for words that "fit" your subject. Then shape them into a poem.

Make a list.

Find your favorite words in the nest, and list them in order. List all the weather words or the "W" words or the color words. See what unique and surprising groupings you can use to create a nestling.

3. Play with words.

Just like birds build their nests with whatever is available to them—straw, shoelaces, paper, mud!   you, too, can be inventive. Here are some ways to find unique and surprising nestlings:

Use verbs as nouns or nouns as verbs.
For instance, the word "puddle" is used is a noun in "Nest," but I used it as a verb in the nestling "Miracle."

Press words together to create your own unique words.
Some words I created were *wordflight*, *frostsong*, *skyboat*. You'll know when words belong together by the way they sound and by the image they create in your mind. (This is one of my favorite nest-building tricks!)

Be on the lookout for sneaky words.
Sometimes wonderful words will hide inside other (longer) words. When I found "butter" in "butterfly" and "ink" in "wrinkly," I couldn't wait to place them in nestlings.

Use your title.
Because your word choice is limited in the body of the nestling, you can create a title to help position the reader or to add information or context. For instance, in the Space Poems section I could have titled my nestling "Pluto," but a more effective title is "On Pluto No Longer Being Named a Planet."

4. Nurture your nestlings.

Ask yourself:
Does this poem make me feel something? Does it offer a surprising image or analogy? Does it engage the senses? What does it mean? Allow the answers to these questions to guide you in revision.

Check and double-check the order of your words.
The order in which the words appear is really the only hard-and-fast rule about creating nestlings. Make sure you're accurate.

Go back to the nest.
Are there any words that would help make your poem stronger, or create a different meaning? Alternately, are there words better left out? Now is your chance to use only the best words for your poem!

Experiment with placement of the words on the page.
Try different line breaks, indentation, and spacing. Think about which words you want the reader to linger on. Use punctuation or white space to help make that happen.

5. Fly!
The best part about nest-building and finding nestlings is sending them out into the world and watching them fly. You can share your nestlings with a friend by writing them on a piece of paper, by creating works of art, or simply by reading them aloud.

As you open your heart to this experience, I hope you will find that there is nothing more joyful than discovering yourself and the world in a poem-nest.

You—yes, you—

are a poet

and

a poem!

–IL, January 5, 2020

INDEX OF POEM TITLES

(Apologies to X and Z upon Not Being Included in the Index)

What fate:
shut off,
no tune for you—

world turns,
clouds rattle—

despite chill,
both
           now inside